Numerology
Made Easy

D1311389

Numerology
Made Easy

Hilary H. Carter

BOOKS

Winchester, UK
Washington, USA

First published by O-Books, 2012
O-Books is an imprint of John Hunt Publishing Ltd., Laurel House, Station Approach,
Alresford, Hants, SO24 9JH, UK
office1@o-books.net
www.o-books.com

For distributor details and how to order please visit the 'Ordering' section on our website.

Text copyright: Hilary H. Carter 2010

ISBN: 978 1 84694 717 9

A CIP catalogue record for this book is available from the British Library.

Design: Lee Nash

Printed in the UK by CPI Antony Rowe
Printed in the USA by Offset Paperback Mfrs, Inc

We operate a distinctive and ethical publishing philosophy in all
areas of our business, from our global network of authors to
production and worldwide distribution.

CONTENTS

'When times are mysterious,
Serious numbers will always be heard.'
Paul Simon (When numbers get serious)

CHAPTER ONE

NUMBERS IN YOUR LIFE

Numbers are everywhere. Right now, wherever you are, reading these words, look around and you will see numbers. This page is numbered, as are pages in all books. Look on the back cover of this book and you will see it has been assigned a number. All books are identified by this number, known as the ISBN.

We live in a mathematical world. We live in a world of time and space, both of which are measured by number. Wherever you go, the distance is measured in numbers. From centimetres to kilometres, from inches to miles, the space between two locations is numbered. Roads have a number, as do the houses on the road. Earth itself is numbered by latitude and longitude.

Time is measured according to numbers too. We have 60 seconds in a minute, 60 minutes in an hour, 24 hours in a day. That is the case wherever you live in the world. Number is at the basis of our everyday life. We know what age we are as the passage of time is measured in numbers. We also have 'special numbers' such as coming of age at 18 or 21 or reaching the milestone of 100 years.

From the moment you are born, you are numbered. Your day, month and year of birth all have a number assigned to them. On your birth certificate you will have your own personal number. You'll have a tax number, a national insurance number, a passport number, a driving license number, a bank account number and a telephone number. Go shopping and your checkout will be numbered, as will virtually all the food you buy. Look at the bar codes and you will see that each item you buy is numbered. You might pay with cash which will have numbers inscribed (coins) or printed (notes) on it or you might pay by bank card which will have its own unique number. You will then have to enter your pin number to pay.

It's just endless. Numbers are deeply ingrained into our everyday life and most people just accept that as a fact and don't think any further about number.

But do numbers have any significance beyond being used to identify or measure something or someone? I believe they do. Numbers are beyond words. They are pure manifestation of energy. They speak to us in a fascinating and enlightening way and once you have learned how to read this particular language, you will be able to read your world. The appearance of numbers in our everyday lives is not purely random. Numbers are constantly talking to us if we would just stop, listen and take note. By bringing our awareness into the moment we can notice numbers and then we can start to learn the language that they speak.

In this book you will discover the meaning of numbers in your world, explained in a way that is of practical use. The information I am presenting here is based on my own experiences and research into number spanning a period of over twenty five years.

REINCARNATION AND THE REFLECTION PERIOD

Using your name and your date of birth you will be able to find your own personal numbers. We all have different combinations of numbers. Why do you have your particular numbers?

You will see that I refer to previous lives in this book. Some of you will not be familiar with the idea of the soul being born again and again, yet it makes sense that we come to earth many times and that we live many lives. In each life we learn and experience. A life on earth can be likened to a school. At the level of the soul we have stored all the experiences, lessons and emotions of the many lives we have lived.

When the body dies, the consciousness that was in that body

lives on. There are exceptions, but in the normal course of events, at the moment of death, which is when the final breath leaves the body, there is the appearance of a bright white light in the distance. It's a bit like looking at a light at the end of a tunnel. The soul is drawn to that light and there is a feeling of peace. Released from the confines of the physical body, you will have returned to the astral plane, which is simply another level of existence. Death is not at all frightening. It is rather like returning to a familiar and much loved family home after a long journey abroad.

OVERVIEW

After death comes the time of reflection, which I refer to in this book as the overview. There is nobody judging you. There is no pass or fail. There is no punishment. When you feel ready to take an objective look at the life you have just lived, then that is exactly what happens. You get to see the big picture of your life which can be very different to the little picture that we see here on earth.

Reflecting on your current life here on earth on a regular basis is a good idea. You can take time to pause and withdraw from your everyday activities. Take a life audit, looking at the various areas of your life such as work, relationships and hobbies. In this way you can see what is working for you, where you are feeling fulfilled and where changes need to be made. But a life review on earth is minor compared to the overview after death. Looking through clear eyes at the soul on the astral plane, you can see what has been learned, what has manifested as a result of your actions, what you have done to help others, where you have blocked or suppressed yourself or others and what needs to be learned next. It's a bit like end of term exams but you set the exams and you mark them.

After the overview the soul decides where it needs to focus its energy in the next life. With help from guides and teachers on the astral plane, a time and place for the next incarnation is chosen. It's a complex process as the positions of the planets as well as the numbers of the days, months and years need to be taken into account.

You won't normally incarnate again immediately after the overview, though this does sometimes happen. Many of those civilians and soldiers who were killed in the second world war came back very quickly and manifested as the peace loving 1960s generation.

This book aims to shed some light on the numbers that you have chosen in the overview and consequently what soul qualities and lessons you are concentrating on in this life.

CHAPTER TWO

HOW TO USE THIS BOOK

In this book you can discover your 3 main numbers:

1. Your life path number, based on your date of birth.

2. Your karma number, based on the day you were born.

3. Your destiny number based on your name.

THOSE ARE THE THREE NUMBERS THAT ARE PERSONAL TO YOU. HOWEVER, YOU CAN ALSO DISCOVER:

4. How to change your destiny number to help you to develop qualities that you are lacking.

5. The meaning of repeated digits and other number patterns when they appear in your everyday life.

6. How to keep focussed on your life's purpose by creating a life list based on the law of 5.

Using all of the above information can help you to understand yourself and identify your strengths and weaknesses. It can give you greater clarity in this life; where you are heading, what you need to focus on, the lessons you set yourself before incarnating and why you act and react in the way that you do.

You can also work out the numbers of friends and family. Once you understand what makes them tick and what lessons they are working on, hopefully you will be able to be more compassionate and understanding towards them. In that way, knowledge of numerology can be a great help in personal and professional relationships.

This book will also look at the way numbers talk to us through the appearance of repeated digits and number patterns.

Chapters eight and nine shed new light on the enigmatic number 23 and the emerging 11:11 phenomenon.

CHAPTER THREE

FIND YOUR LIFE PATH AND KARMA NUMBER

There are eleven life paths; 1, 2, 3, 4, 5, 6, 7, 8, 9, 11 and 22. Rather like the 12 signs of the zodiac, each of these life paths presents you with certain gifts and challenges. You are only on one of these life paths and it is fixed for the duration of this incarnation. The life path number is derived from your date of birth which your soul will have chosen before incarnating onto earth in order to gain the experiences it needs in this particular life. The life path number is really important because you cannot do anything to change it. You were born on the day that your soul chose to be born and nothing can change that. Even if you were induced, premature or overdue, the day that you drew your first breath is your birth date.

Whatever has been written on your birth certificate as your date of birth is the date that you need to use. If you don't know your date of birth then you won't be able to find your life path.

Calculate your life path number first. This will give you the information that reveals your strengths, weaknesses and your life direction. This number indicates the main focus of your current life. This is the base line of your life and it reveals your core personality. It is the most important of your three numbers.

FIND YOUR LIFE PATH

It's very easy to find your life path. You simply reduce the birth date to a single digit except for the master numbers 11 and 22 which are never reduced. You add up the day, the month and the year separately. Some books might give other ways of adding up your birth date but this is the correct way. Why? Because if you

do not add the 3 numbers (day/month/year) separately you might miss a master number life path. Example one demonstrates this.

EXAMPLE ONE

25th Aug 1969. (25/08/1969 or 08/25/1969)

If we add the numbers separately we have:

2+5=7

0+8=8

1+9+6+9=25. 2+5=7

7+8+7=22. This correct method gives us a master life path of 22.

If we had not added the numbers separately we would have added 2+5+0+8+1+9+6+9=40. 4+0=4.

This incorrect method would have given us a 4 life path.

EXAMPLE TWO

31st December 1988

31/12/1988. (Or 12/31/1988)

3+1=4

1+2=3

1+9+8+8=26. 2+6=8

This needs to be reduced to one digit.4+3+8=15. 1+5=6

So the life path is 6

Remember, the only numbers that we don't reduce are 11 and 22. These are the master numbers and they are more powerful that the numbers 1-9.

EXAMPLE THREE

23/11/1975 (Or 11/23/1975)

2+3=5

11=11

1+9+7+5=22

5+11+22=38. 3+8=11

The 11 is not reduced. This person is on an 11 life path. They're on a Master Number life path.

EXAMPLE FOUR

19/08/1988 (Or 8/19/1988)

1+9=10. 1+0=1

0+8=8

1+9+8+8=26. 2+6=8

1+8+8=17. 1=7=8

The life path is 8. This person will manifest the characteristics of an 8 life path very markedly as not only are they on an 8 life path but their birth date includes three 8's, including a double 8.

EXAMPLE FIVE

22/11/1983 (Or 11/22/1983)

22=22

11=11

1+9+8+3=21. 2+1=3

22+11+3=36. 3+6=9

So the life path is 9. The 11 and 22 were not reduced.

EXAMPLE SIX

24th May 1972.

24/05/1972 (Or 05/24/1972)

2+4=6

0+5=5

1+9+7+2=19 1+9=10 1+0=1

Add those numbers up.6+5+1=12. 1+2=3

So the life path is 3.

That's it. It's that easy! You now have your life path number. Turn to chapter 5 or 6 and read the relevant number. Remember that although this life path number is very important, it needs to be read in conjunction with the numbers within your name, known as the destiny number. The numbers in your name modify the energy of the life path. If your life path is a safe and steady number four but your name is full of slightly wild and changeable fives, then you will have both of these qualities in your personality. Turn to the chapter 4 to discover your destiny number.

YOUR KARMA NUMBER

The karma number is based on the day that you were born. As with the life path, this number is fixed for the duration of this life. Use the following chart to discover your karma number.

EXAMPLE

If you were born on 5th of a month, your karma number is 5.

If you were born on 17th of a month, your karma number is 8.

If you were born on 11th of a month, your karma number is 11.

(Remember, 11 and 22 are not reduced to a single digit).

DAY OF MONTH / YOUR KARMA NUMBER

1st /1

2nd /2

3rd /3

4th /4

5th /5

6th /6

7th /7

8th /8

9th /9

10th /1

11th /11

12th /3

13th /4* (see below)

14th /5

15th /6

16th /7

17th /8* (see below)

18th /9

19th /1* (see below)

20th /2

21st /3

22nd /22

23rd /5

24th /6

25th /7

26th /8

27th /9

28th /1

29th /11

30th /3

31st /4

The karma number is secondary to the life path number. To find out the meaning of your karma number, look at the strengths and weaknesses list under the relevant number in chapter 5 (numbers 1-9) or chapter 6 (numbers 11 and 22). The weaknesses indicate which negative character traits you are trying to overcome in this life. The strengths indicate the potential gifts that each number bestows on you.

EXAMPLE

*Dawn was born on 14th May 1991. Her life path is a 3. (1+4=**5**. 5=**5**. 1+9+9+1=20=**2**. 5+5+2=12. 1+2=3). By reading LIFE PATH THREE in chapter 5 Dawn discovers what her soul is working on and why she has chosen that path. She was born on 14th. Her karma number is 5. She now reads 'strengths and weaknesses' under number 5. This reveals her sub lesson.*

*There are three special karma numbers; 13, 17 and 19. If you were born on any of those dates you have chosen to carry an extra karmic debt in this life.

Those choosing to incarnate on 13th of any month (4*) are bringing in extra stuff to deal with in this life. This extra karma that they are choosing to pay off is normally of a personal nature. They will be brought in contact with people and situations that they need to resolve to clear the way for progress in their next life.

Those choosing the 17th of any month (8*) bring in even more extra karma than the 13th. The soul wants to shift spiritually and they feel ready to deal with people and situations that have proven very difficult in previous lives. Thus they can find themselves in relationships with the very people that they find the most difficult. If you have experienced a bitter divorce in this life or if you hold bitterness and resentment to a former boss or your husband's/wife's lovers, be aware that these are the very people you might give birth to or marry in your next life! You'll have to forgive them at some point so maybe it would be better to forgive them now.

The 19th of any month (1*) is the ultimate karmic choice. Here is the soul who wishes to atone for just about everything they deem necessary. In the overview they have normally experienced such remorse for their actions in previous lives that they simply want to come back to earth to put things right. They want to re-dress the balance. 19 people actually take on more than simply personal karma. The 19's of a high consciousness can quite literally offer their lives as a sacrifice. These lives can prove very difficult. Often there is a make or break quality about their lives. They find themselves in 'sink or swim' situations but out of these difficulties and challenges can manifest greater good.

Please note that the karmic 13/17/19 is solely for those born on 13th/17th/19th of a month and is not derived from adding up the birth date.

CHAPTER FOUR

THE DESTINY NUMBER

The life path number forms the base line for this life. However, this cannot be taken in isolation. We human beings are not quite that simple! We need also to calculate the destiny number. The destiny number is much more flexible than the life path number. This is based on the full name that you were given at birth.

Words have energy. You only have to look at the work of Masaru Emoto to see how true that statement is. Emoto exposed water to different words. He then froze the water and took photos of the resulting crystals. Water that had been exposed to beautiful works such as 'love, harmony and peace' produced balanced and harmonious crystals. Water that had been sworn at produced ugly, imbalanced crystals.

Names have an energy associated with them. Your name is your label and it's attached to you along with the energy of that name. That, in turn, comes from the number resonance.

You can change the energy that's attached to you by changing the spelling of your name or even changing your name altogether. Sometimes that just happens, for example through adoption or marriage. Or you may consciously choose to change your name.

Changes in your name have a subtle effect on you. What has actually happened through the name change is that you have changed your number resonance.

CHOOSING A NAME
Some parents have a name lined up long before a baby is even conceived. Others spend months trying to decide on a name and as soon as they see the baby a name pops into their head. The

parents then wonder where on earth that name came from! Some people might wish to choose a baby's name according to the numerological status of the name.

"Let's give her a 22 vibration so she'll be a powerful force in the world."

Or "Let's make his name add up to 5 so he'll be able to cope with our nomadic lifestyle."

But really, the soul has already chosen his/her name in the overview and even if you take this calculated approach, the baby will receive the name it has chosen before incarnation. Do you think you chose the name of your children? I don't!

The energy of the family name (surname) will be running throughout the family. Families also tend to have names that are repeated through the generations. "We called him Robert after his grandfather". This indicates the same energy being worked on by the family tree through the generations.

Whatever the baby is called and however the name is decided upon, once it is written on the birth certificate that name becomes the official name and that is the name that you will be using to find the destiny number. Even if you were adopted soon after birth or were never known by the name on your birth certificate, you use this name to calculate your name numerology. Use ALL the names you were given at birth, even if you were named after all the members of a football team. (It does happen.)

DESTINY NUMBER

Remember, your destiny number is your name number.

It's very easy to find out your destiny number. Each letter is given a number as shown in the following chart.

ALPHABET CHART

A	B	C	D	E	F	G	H	I
1	2	3	4	5	6	7	8	9

J	K	L	M	N	O	P	Q	R
1	2	3	4	5	6	7	8	9

S	T	U	V	W	X	Y	Z
1	2	3	4	5	6	7	8

This is the classic way of numbering the letters, where A=1, B=2, C=3 and so on. It is based on our current 26 letter alphabet. This is the one that I use and I find it very accurate. There are other letter/number systems used by some numerologists based on ancient alphabets, but I feel that as we are living in the 21st century, the 21st century alphabet is the relevant one to use. This book is a straightforward guide to numerology. If you decide to delve more deeply into the subject you can explore and experiment with the other systems for yourself.

- *The destiny number describes your potential. Your soul wants to develop the positive attributes of this number in this life. This number is calculated using all the letters in your name.*

- *The destiny number and the karma number differ because, unlike the karma number, the destiny number can be changed by changing your name.*

How do you discover the secrets of the numbers hidden within your name? Follow these examples:

EXAMPLE ONE

SOPHIA RAMSAY BREWSTER

Sophia was given 3 names at birth. Sophia is her personal name. Ramsay is her mother's family name and Brewster is her father's family name. All 3 names appear on her birth certificate. These are the only names that appear on her birth certificate. If there were 7 names we would use all 7. We assign a number to each letter using the alphabet chart above.

Each name is calculated separately.

Sophia: 1+6+7+8+9+1=32. 3+2= (5)

Ramsay: 9+1+4+1+1+7=23. 2+3= (5)

Brewster: 2+9+5+5+1+2+5+9=38. 3+8= (11) (not reduced)

5+5+11=21 2+1=3 That gives a destiny number of 3.

Sophia now turns to chapter 5 and reads about the strengths and weaknesses within her destiny number 3. She reads this in conjunction with her life path number.

EXAMPLE TWO

JOHN WINSTON LENNON

John: 1+6+8+5=20=(2)

Winston: 5+9+5+1+2+6+5=33=(6)

Lennon: 3+5+5+5+6+5=29=(11)

2+6+11=19. 1+9=10 1+0=**1**

So his destiny number is 1. Number one is about newness. Along with the other Beatles he was in the forefront of a radical change in modern music.

However, the 5 influence is quite strong. It is always worth noting when a number is repeated many times within a name or a birth date. Look at how many times a '5' letter appears in his name. 5 is the communicator and he was certainly a messenger whilst here on earth.

EXAMPLE THREE

WILLIAM BLAKE

William=5+9+3+3+9+1+4=34=3+4=(7)

Blake=2+3+1+2+5=13=1+3=(4)

7+4=11

William Blake has an 11 destiny number. He is an example of an 11 who managed to fulfil the potential of his master number.

CHANGING YOUR DESTINY NUMBER

This is where knowledge of numbers and their energies can aid you in taking control of your destiny.

EXAMPLE

Nicola was on a 5 life path and was a multi talented young woman. She was an artist and a dress designer. However, one of her main weaknesses was not completing things. She wanted to start her own clothes label but she lacked staying power, the type of energy that grounds things and allows them to manifest. The best number for that is the number 4. So how can Nicola bring the energy of the number 4 into her life?

Nicola has no middle name. Her birth certificate gives her name as Nicola Hanson.

DESTINY NUMBER

Nicola=5+9+3+6+3+1=27 2+7=9

Hanson=8+1+5+1+6+5=26 2+6=8

Her destiny number is 9+8=17 1+7=8

Letters to the value of 4 do not appear anywhere in her name. How can she change that and bring the much needed qualities of 4 into her life? There are 4 ways:

1. Add a name to her existing name.

2. Change the spelling of her name.

3. Add an initial.

4. Change her name.

1: ADD A NAME

Looking at the alphabet chart you can see that the letters that carry the 4 vibration are D, M and V. Using those 3 letters Nicola could create a middle name 'VADIM' and be known as Nicola Vadim Hanson. That's a perfectly good name for an artist/ designer and provides Nicola with 3x4's.

In addition to gaining 3x4's, Nicola's destiny number will now change to a 3.

Nicola=5+9+3+6+3+1=27 2+7=9

Vadim=4+1+4+9+4=22

Hanson=8+1+5+1+6+5=26 2+6=8

Her destiny number is now 9+22+8=39=12=3

2: CHANGE SPELLING

Using the name Nicola Hanson, her destiny number is 8. To convert that to a 4 she needs to add a letter somewhere in her name that has the value '5', as 8+5=13=4. E, N and W have the value 5. It would be easy to spell Hanson as Hansone thereby changing her name resonance to a '4'. Or adding an extra 'n' to Hannson would have the same effect. It's a subtle change that's very easy to put into practise in everyday life.

Nicola=5+9+3+6+3+1=27 2+7=9

Hansone=8+1+5+1+6+5+5=31=4

Her destiny number is now 9+4=13 1+3=4

OR:

Nicola=5+9+3+6+3+1=27 2+7=9

Hannson=8+1+5+5+1+6+5=31=4

Her destiny number is now 9+4=13 1+3=4

3: ADD AN INITIAL

Adding E, N or W as a middle initial (Nicola N. Hanson) would have a more powerful effect as it would change her resonance to the master number 22. She could choose this option if she felt she could carry this powerful vibration within her new name.

Nicola =5+9+3+6+3+1=27 2+7=9

E (or N or W) =5

Hanson= 8+1+5+1+6+5=26 2+6=8

Her destiny number is 9+5+8=22

4: CHANGE NAME

This is the most radical option. It is also the most difficult so think carefully before you embark on this option. Changing your whole name will certainly change your resonance but it might not be necessary if you use one of the above methods instead.

If Nicola came to me for a numerology reading I would actually suggest that she could use 'Vadim' as the name for her fashion label. Not only does 'Vadim' contain 3x4's, it also adds up to 22 which is a master number. So she could choose for her collection to be known simply as VADIM, but only if she felt that her fashion designs could manage to carry the high energetic vibration of the 22 as VADIM = 4+1+4+9+4=22.

KNOWN NAMES

You might have been named Matilda Apple Germaine Catherine Delmonte Jones, but if you are known as Matty Jones, or if you always use the name Matilda Delmonte, then work out the numerology for the name that you actually use. The destiny number (based on the full name given at birth) is the underlying resonance that you chose before birth. However, as life progresses, we change and so can our names. We frequently become known by names other than our birth names.

Helen was named Helen Susan Platten at birth.
She was adopted at 6 weeks and her name was completely changed to Rachel Christine Jones.
She married at 18 and her name changed to Rachel Christine Munton.
When she was 32 that marriage ended in divorce. She remarried and then became known as Rachel Christine Walker.

Work out the numerology for your present name and discover your current destiny number.

NICK NAMES

It's fun to play around with names. You might have a formal name but if your partner always refers to you as 'Bubblekin' or your mother calls you 'Billybong', then work out the numbers for your nickname and discover what energy is resonating between the two of you!

COMPANY NAMES

You can also calculate the numbers in the name of a company or a business. Using your knowledge of numbers you can choose a company name that carries the appropriate energy. For example, a beauty salon might want to choose a 6 vibration. A communications company might feel that a 5 vibration would suit them.

PLACE NAMES

Place names have their own number resonance. London, for example, is an eleven. New York is a three. Work out the number of your own town.

CHAPTER FIVE

LIFE PATHS ONE TO NINE

LIFE PATH ONE

Number one, not surprisingly, is about beginnings. Normally the soul will choose a number one life path when the previous life has been one in which a lot of loose ends have been tied up. The life immediately before this one has often been a chaotic and fragmented life. Now the soul is ready to start on a new phase. It's a bit like ending a chapter and turning the page for a new chapter. Or even finishing one book and starting a new book. One is quite an important life path because whatever is done in this life will lay the foundations for the next sequence of lives.

In this life the soul wants to establish a direction for the future. It does not follow that the life paths are chosen in numerological order (1 then 2 then 3 etc.) but on a one life path there is always the energy of 'newness' the ability to make a fresh start or bring something new into the world.

This life path offers the soul greater clarity of vision than any of the other ten paths. Think of something being brand new and unused. That's the feeling of a one life path. The soul is as yet unhindered and has just off-loaded a lot of baggage. That feeling of freedom and lightness can often still be felt even though the soul is now living in the physical realm. It's a fresh, 'raring to go' energy.

Some number ones leave their mark as inventors or founders of all sorts of things including such diverse things as founding an orphanage, establishing a company or even inventing something. The one is creative. But new chapters, new creations and new inventions don't have to be massive or famous. Sometimes the number one will spend this lifetime changing their ways of thinking, leaving behind patterns of being and living that have been ingrained in their soul for ages. They are renewing their thought patterns and founding a new way of approaching life.

If you look at the number '1' it is almost indistinguishable from the letter 'I' and this clearly indicates the main danger that a one life path can fall into, namely that of egotism and self-centredness. Ones don't like it when they're not in charge because they prefer to be leaders rather than followers. If you've chosen a one life path you need to learn that you cannot always be first.

Ones are strong and determined but they don't always stick at things. They like to initiate but the block to rapid progress of their soul is their tendency not to complete what they start. There is no point in being an inventor if your invention remains in the mind and never becomes manifest.

Although a lot of baggage from previous lives has been left behind just prior to this incarnation, it's very easy to pick up a new load. Visualise what your home is like when you've just had a big clear out. Getting rid of unused gifts, unworn clothes and unwanted possessions leaves a house beautifully clear, but after a few weeks or months the clutter can soon return and the house can be back to where it started. Only regularly and strictly controlling what is brought into the house can keep it clear. So it is with those on this particular life path. They need to be wary of slipping backwards into negative thought patterns and ways of being. Regular life reviews need to take place.

If you are on a one life path, look carefully at your life and, using your ability to see clearly, try to be objective in your overview of your motives for your actions. The world needs people who can initiate, but the greatest reward from being on this life path will come from initiating for the good of all, not for the good of self. Always look to the motives behind your actions.

And ponder on this question; what is the difference between independence and self-centredness?

RELATIONSHIPS

Regarding relationships, I have noticed that often these people are loners. Sometimes this is through choice but more often it is circumstances that isolate them. It is as if they cannot easily manage to find a mate, that fate deals them the lonesome card, but it could be that subconsciously, staying solo keeps the number one clear to create and do as they wish. Even if they do find a partner, these people will always have an independent streak.

If you are in a relationship with a one then be aware of their need to be in charge. Strangely, although they can be bossy, they have serious issues with dependency versus independence. They can become very needy in relationships. One of their lessons is to learn to stand on their own two feet and function as an individual.

THE ONE CHILD

If you are raising a one child then give them plenty of opportunities to play group sports or other group activities. In this way they can learn to co-operate with others. However, they need to be in charge of something so give them a responsible task such as being in charge of feeding the dog or collecting and sorting the mail.

DESTINY NUMBER ONE

STRENGTHS

Leadership abilities, creative, organized, daring, ambitious, energetic, air of authority, clarity of vision, inventive, brave, independent, inventive, positive, determined.

WEAKNESSES

Selfish, pushy, arrogant, the bully, self centred, tactless, unfeeling, lack of compassion, egocentric, bossy, 'me-first' attitude.

LIFE PATH TWO

Number two is the number of duality. On this life path the soul is choosing to look in the mirror and what better way is there of doing that than being in a relationship? In relationships the soul has its unconscious self reflected in others. All the emotions, patterns, behaviour, prejudices, fears, worries, likes and dislikes that have previously been 'stuffed' and hidden can be brought to light on a two life path.

This is not the easiest life path to choose for the soul is bringing to light that stuff that it has previously decided is too difficult to face. In the overview the soul will have recognised its tendency to keep a lid on its emotions and feelings and it will have chosen a two life path in order to begin to open up. Souls on a two life path are here to learn to co-operate with other people such as co-workers, children, friends and partners.

This can be a very rewarding life as huge psychological leaps can be made for the soul who is willing to rise to the challenge. Twos make excellent counsellors as they are not usually judgemental and they are able to empathise. Their humanitarian nature is a huge asset in any work involving charity.

A two who is on track will be contentedly working behind the scenes within a group, coming up with ideas that other members of the group will bring to fruition. A two will be happy to accept the satisfaction of his ideas being manifest without any personal acclaim. They will bring a sense of harmony to any endeavour they are involved in.

Normally a two will be quite happy to play second fiddle. They seek to please others. Their patience and concern for the welfare of others makes them highly thought of, though they do not tend to think of themselves highly.

If a two is expressing negatively, their excess nervous energy can cause emotional problems. They can become seriously indecisive resulting in the inability to get anything off the ground because as they don't know what decision to make, they don't make one at all! Their self worth can be very low and they can too easily put the needs of others above their own causing stress, overwork and the resulting health problems.

Twos are sensitive souls and sometimes they will find life all a bit too much and will want to retreat to a place where they do not have to face their unconscious demons. They may decide to live in isolation which would be against the urge of the soul. In that situation they are just running away from purpose of this life path. If you are a two who has retreated I'd urge you to have courage to come out of hiding.

RELATIONSHIPS

If you are in a relationship with a two then you will need to return the love and affection that the two will offer you. They can become very co-dependent within a relationship and are hyper sensitive to emotional rejection. They are usually happy to take second place and often allow themselves to be dominated. They seek peace and harmony. If the two is married, the partner is often a soul mate.

THE TWO CHILD

If you are raising a two child then you need to work on building their confidence. They will need gentle handling because of their sensitivity. It would not be a good idea to throw them into 'rough and tumble' situations to toughen them up. Their nervous system is finely tuned so they tend not to be as robust as their peers. Give them opportunities to play host/hostess. Let them make cakes with you and invite a friend to tea or invite one or two of their friends over to their house to make dens.

DESTINY NUMBER TWO

STRENGTHS
Patient, tolerant, quiet, peaceful, forgiving, diplomatic, peace maker, balanced and fair, mediator, friendly, charming, diplomatic, good host/hostess, considerate, reliable, good at handling people.

WEAKNESSES
Shy, lack of direction, no zest for life, spineless, vague, easily led, no ambition, too sensitive to the opinions of others, excess nervous energy, indecisive, petty.

LIFE PATH THREE

Number three takes the soul into contact with its own Divinity. Three is the number of trinity; Father, Son and Holy Ghost / Yin, Yang and Tao / Positive, negative and neutral.

Mathematically the number three takes us into the realm of matter for here we have the formation of the triangle, the three sided figure. This life path is about synthesis, bringing Divinity into matter. Often the souls who choose a three life path have recently emerged from a past life devoid of spirituality and have now chosen to explore their Divine consciousness. Choosing this life path the soul is moving towards understanding its place and purpose in the greater whole. They are here to learn that Divinity is not 'out there' but is within everything that exists. Although seven is said to be the spiritual number, in fact three can be deeply spiritual.

In their positive expression, threes are wonderful company. They are charming hosts and hostesses, often talented in the arts, especially theatre. Their own lives can be theatrical, especially in regard to relationships. They are warm and sociable and have a sunny disposition. They can be talkative (or at least communicative) but they are great listeners too.

The two main pitfalls for a three are fanaticism or being ungrounded. Threes are sometimes drawn to religions and belief systems. If the three chooses to follow the path of religion then they will need to tread carefully, taking one step at a time rather than leaping feet first into a fringe movement or radical religion. Pause, examine and reflect would be the key words of advice for a three.

The second great danger is that of not being grounded. Threes can be too much in the head and are prone to being easily led. That is why a spiritual discipline is so important on this particular life path. Sitting meditation is not the best form for these souls. Walking or moving meditation would be better because it incorporates the body with the mind and spirit. They need to combine their prayer/meditation/divinity directly with the physical body. To support their need to keep in balance on this life path it is quite important for the three to take up a physical spiritual discipline such as Tai Chi, martial arts or Yoga. Without such practices the three can be prone to huge swings in their moods, from high to low and back again. A three in balance will be level headed and emotionally stable. Out of balance, watch out!

A three who has lost their way will be living a shallow life centred on their own desires. They might have become moody, withdrawing into silence whenever their ego is bruised by comments and actions of others. They will suffer from highs and lows rather than being balanced and steady. They have a strong tendency to escapism, either through drugs and drink or by becoming a rolling stone.

RELATIONSHIPS

In relationships, the three is an ardent and loyal partner. They tend to be very giving so they need to be wary of bowing too low to the demands of others and becoming a doormat. If you are in relationship with a three then you need to make sure that the give and take within the relationship is kept in balance. Although the three tends to be very popular with the opposite sex, once committed they are loyal. Threes have dreams and visions for the future. A wise partner will support the three in these.

THE THREE CHILD

If you are raising a three child, try and give them a piece of land to cultivate. Even a window box will do. Teach them to use the earth to grow edible plants. Any activity involving the earth, such as gardening, pottery or walking in nature will help them to ground. If you are a city dweller, make sure your child has access to a sand tray. A three child would benefit from drama club. Let them play out their dramatic side on the stage rather than at home. Give them plenty of opportunities to mix with other children.

DESTINY NUMBER THREE

STRENGTHS

Charming, sociable, theatrical, musical, good taste, bubbly, artistically talented, attractive, sexy, expressive, entertaining, articulate and witty, romantic, popular, creative.

WEAKNESSES

Vain, domineering, promiscuous, critical, impatient, fickle, shallow, flirty, indulgent, pleasure seeking, always wanting to be in the limelight, jealous, prone to addictions.

LIFE PATH FOUR

'Four square' is an expression that means firm, steady and unwavering. These are the key words for the soul who has chosen a four life path. Another interpretation of 'four square' is to be forthright, frank or blunt.

These are the souls who can be described as salt of the earth. In mathematics four is represented by the square. A soul on a four life path is often found in a situation where they are blocked or restricted in some way, as though they are inside that square and cannot get out. The lesson here is to learn to live in harmony with restriction.

These people are the builders of the universe. Just as those on the 22 life path are referred to as Master Builders, the four is referred to simply as the builder. In this life they have the opportunity to create or establish something concrete in the physical universe. Often the previous life has been excessively idealistic. Maybe the soul was full of ideas that remained as ideas, nothing came of those ideas. The ideas would have died with the person when the body died. The overview of the previous life would have prompted the soul to want to create on the physical plane, to leave something concrete behind when they die this time round. I'm not saying that they all literally want to build buildings (though that is one manifestation of this life path) but the purpose of choosing a four path is to get the ideas out of their head and into the world.

Fours make great friends as they tend to prefer to have a few good friends rather than lots of more superficial relationships. They are patient and determined and that gives them the ability to see things through to the end.

People can take advantage of the dependable nature of a four, resulting in them being used. They need to learn to stand up for themselves.

The main danger of a four is inherent in their solid nature.

33

The square is very solid and stable but the down side is that the soul can become stuck or stubborn. That's why they can get stuck in unfulfilling relationships, staying in a marriage devoid of love because they lack the drive to leave and move on. They might stay in the same job for years and miss out on opportunities to branch out in other directions. Although they are capable and organised, they can have very fixed ideas and will not always listen to the opinions of others. They have a tendency to block input (often very valuable and helpful input) from others.

Conversely, the four might rebel against any restrictions imposed upon them. In doing so, they can create chaos. The four needs to tread that fine line between accepting restriction and not getting stuck.

This soul will make the most progress on this path if they can learn to be more open and less fixed. It takes courage to move on or to embrace change, but sometimes it's the right thing to do.

RELATIONSHIPS

In relationships the four will usually be loyal and will stand by their partner through thick and thin, even if in some cases the relationship has died and is void of feelings. The same is true with their friendships. If you're in a relationship with a four then you have a partner you can depend on. They will be there for you in a practical way. They can become a bit too dependent on their partner so you'll need to make sure that you both have a life outside of the relationship. Encourage your partner to do things without you as well as with you.

THE FOUR CHILD

If you are raising a four child then give them plenty of opportunities to build with clay, play-dough, wood or sand. Any activities involving team work would be helpful to these souls. Team sports or any physical activity that demands flexibility of the body (e.g. gymnastics) will help them to learn to flow and adapt to life more easily.

DESTINY NUMBER FOUR

STRENGTHS
Loyal, steady, hard working, methodical, practical, patient, reliable, logical, proud, dependable, solid, honest, sincere, salt of the earth.

WEAKNESSES
Too serious, depressive, mean, stubborn, crude, tight fisted, didactic, boring, sluggish, slow and plodding, clinging, immovable, fearful, stuck, suffocating.

LIFE PATH FIVE

Number five is a very interesting life path to undertake. This is the number of freedom. Here is the soul who has normally spent many, many lives being restricted in some way. They might have repeatedly chosen to take holy orders, removing themselves from the world and hiding behind the high walls of an institution. Or their lack of freedom might have been less physical by being imposed by a belief system whereby the soul has lived its life (lives) according to strict rules and regulations. These rules would have denied the soul the freedom to explore in all ways; dietary restrictions, the inability to physically travel, the mind closed to other ways of thinking. By choosing a five life path the soul is ready to break down the mental and physical barriers that have prevented it from expressing the total freedom that is its birthright.

These people often become communicators in some form. In the magic square of 15 (see page 71) it can be seen that 5 is the central number. This is the ONLY number in the square that has connection with ALL the other numbers from 1-9. Being in contact with all numbers is indicative of the way the soul can relate in this life. They are usually able to get on with people from all walks of life. That's what makes them good teachers, journalists, writers and communicators. They love to travel, explore and experience other ways of living.

The five hates to be tied down. Routine, boredom and the feeling of being trapped, both literally and figuratively, are the things that will cause immense frustration to a restless five. 'Multi' is the key word for a five. They benefit from having more than one of everything.

A five who is on track will speak several languages, have more than one job, have friends of both sexes outside of marriage, have a home in two different countries (or a home which is sub-let to someone else) and will enjoy various hobbies.

The main danger of a number five being off track is that of being scattered. These souls, having freed their minds from rigid thinking, can find themselves drawn in many directions. The world can be their oyster and they are often multi-talented. Yet being talented in many areas is more difficult than being talented in one discipline. The five often finds itself with a finger in too many pies and then fails to take anything to fruition. The lesson here is to learn to stay focussed for long enough to take things to their final conclusion. I'm not suggesting staying focussed on one thing throughout life because the five needs to have several things going on in their life at once, but every so often they need to step back and look at their life to see what they have achieved. I always suggest that a five person keeps a list of five goals. This list needs to identify the five most pressing goals in their life and is a useful aid to keeping them focussed and helping them to make the most of their life. (see Chapter 10)

RELATIONSHIPS

'He who binds to himself a joy, does the winged life destroy. But he who kisses the joy as it flies, lives in eternity's sun rise.'

William Blake could have written that for you, if you are lucky enough to have an entertaining, interesting and talented five as a partner. You would be wise to let the five fly like that butterfly. Given freedom of expression, the five will be a stimulating and interesting partner, but try to hold them back then they will become frustrated and likely to stray away in search of new pastures. They are capable of being loyal as long as you don't try and control them. Trust them and they will be trustworthy. Doubt them and they will break free.

THE FIVE CHILD

If you are raising a five child then it would be a good idea to give them the opportunity to run free and feel the wind in their hair. Take them to the top of a hill or to the edge of the sea and let them run unhindered. This will allow the soul to taste the freedom that they have denied themselves so often in the past. Try and choose a school that allows a lot of freedom of expression rather than a strict, heavily disciplined school.

DESTINY NUMBER FIVE

STRENGTHS

Interesting, well informed, lively in body and mind, adventurous, good conversationalist, forward thinking, multi-talented, enthusiastic, good sense of humour, excellent communicator, spontaneous, analytical, compassionate and brave.

WEAKNESSES

Rejects routine, too happy go lucky, unreliable, impulsive,

changeable, fickle, not always loyal, sarcastic, devious, irresponsible, doesn't finish what they start, lacks direction, inconsistent, confused, difficult to pin down, irritable, restless.

LIFE PATH SIX

Number six is traditionally linked to the planet Venus. The key words for the six life path are therefore very like the astrological key words for Venus: love, harmony, peace, beauty and relationship.

The soul on a six life path is endeavouring to bring beauty and love into the world. This can be manifested at many different levels. You could find a six working in all sorts of places, from the assistant on the make-up counter to the landscape artist, from the marriage counsellor to the peace activist. When expressing positively, the nature of a six is very giving. That's what they're working on in this life. They want to create a better and more harmonious world. People who need help and support are instinctively drawn towards the six.

Very often this soul has come directly from a life of violence and discord. It is not uncommon for the soul to have been killed in war in their last life.

Or a soul will often choose the six life path if they have been responsible for the desecration of nature or at least have been disconnected or careless of nature. They choose to redress the damage of the prior life by creating things of beauty in this life. Sometimes they themselves are the creation and the six will go to some lengths to present themselves in the best possible light. They can be willing to go under the knife of the plastic surgeon in their quest for the perfection of beauty. Gardening, home decoration, writing and art are the directions in which the six might be drawn.

Sixes have high standards and they seek perfection, leading

to a state of dissatisfaction when these standards are not reached. This can make them critical, dissatisfied and judgemental.

Sixes who are out of balance can find themselves being treated as a doormat, a slave to the wants, needs and demands of others. Needy and not so needy will lean on an off track six leaving the six feeling burdened. They will be unhappy in this role and can react by becoming mean and moody.

If they have gone the opposite way and opted out of responsibility altogether they will feel a sense of guilt as their conscience will nag at them.

A six who is on track will find themselves in situations of responsibility, giving help and comfort to others. They will have learned to discern between those who genuinely need their help and those who are 'users'. They will therefore choose only to support the weak and vulnerable. They can be very successful in the arts.

RELATIONSHIPS

Relationships are of particular importance to them and a solo six will rarely be content. They need a partner to support their need to be needed! They are willing to give and take within a relationship. Their focus is usually on the home and family and their homes will be warm and welcoming. Their urge to protect their loved ones can go overboard and manifest as 'smother-love'. They love peace and harmony and will go out of their way to keep things balanced and fair so they make great partners. However, their loyalty can extend to staying in dead relationships rather than rocking the boat by leaving.

THE SIX CHILD

If you are raising a six child then plenty of opportunities for creative activities (in their broadest sense) should be offered to the child, from dancing to painting, from dressing up to singing lessons. A dressing up box will allow the six child to explore different persona through imaginative role play.

DESTINY NUMBER SIX

STRENGTHS

Charming, spiritual, peace loving, creative, honest, graceful, serene, humanitarian, loving, caring and thoughtful, sympathetic, home maker, charming and considerate.

WEAKNESSES

Self righteous, extravagant, nosey, meddling, a gossip, interfering in others affairs, vain, cynical, self righteous, needy, mean.

LIFE PATH SEVEN

Number seven life path is always referred to as the spiritual life path, probably because of the spiritual connotations of the number seven. There are many references to number seven in sacred texts, not least in the bible.

There is a sensitivity of heart on a seven life path. These souls are choosing to re-balance the heart in this life. The previous life has often been one where their heart has been damaged in some way, either by being too hard-hearted or too soft-hearted. Having suffered the pain of a broken heart in the last life, the soul is seeking to re-build the structure of the heart. Or having closed off the heart and being too hardened to others, thereby causing them great pain, in this life the heart centre needs to be opened.

It's a case of getting the balance back into the heart area. Hard hearted people have often become that way through over-sensitivity. They have over protected the heart so that they can't feel pain, but in doing so they have closed it down. So by choosing the seven life path the soul is being given the opportunity to build a balanced heart centre. Those on this life path often choose to become quite spiritual as a way of balancing the heart. Surrendering to a higher power or getting in touch with one's own divinity are safe ways of doing this. Unlike conditional human love, Divine love never lets you down, for it is unconditional. It is therefore a safe way to open the heart to love.

A seven who is on track will be analysing the world in a quiet and calm way. They will be working from intuition and using their skills in the outer world by working as a teacher, counsellor or healer. They will not be focussed on the material benefits of their work but on using their fine mind and powers of connection to the spiritual realms in the service of others.

In their positive expression they will be out in the world, quietly confident and sometimes in the public eye. Many sevens choose to express the language of the heart through song or poetry. Other people are uplifted by the energy of a positive seven.

A seven who is off track will have retreated into their own little world, not connecting much with other people and ignoring their spiritual nature. The main danger that faces a seven is the ability to get lost in negativity. They can perceive the world as too harsh to face and will then choose to close themselves into their own shell. They then become unable to either give or to receive.

If you come across a very materialistic seven, then they are not being true to their nature. The seven life path is about choosing to explore the inner landscape. It does not follow that the material world needs to be ignored on this path but it needs to take second place to the spiritual aspect of the soul. Without a connection to the heart and the inner divinity, the life of a seven will lack meaning.

RELATIONSHIPS

In a relationship, the seven is quite difficult to get to know. They tend to keep a lot of their feelings and emotions inside themselves. How can you understand a seven when a seven doesn't understand themself? They operate on a different wavelength to most of us. They can appear cool and aloof but that is only masking inner mental or emotional turmoil. Trust is often an issue for a seven. They don't trust their partner or their partner does not trust them. They find adapting to the ways of others quite difficult which can lead to problems. It is not unusual for a seven to choose to live alone and not be in a relationship at all.

THE SEVEN CHILD

If you are raising a seven child then give them opportunities to love. Buy them a child friendly pet (a gentle, loyal animal) that will give them the unconditional love they need. Allow them to connect with a disadvantaged child through charitable sponsorship. They can learn to give their pocket money to another through love in its wider sense. Allow your seven child to spend time alone without the stimulus of television or other media. Take them to the beach or the forest and let them play and connect with nature.

DESTINY NUMBER SEVEN

STRENGTHS

Kind, psychic, intuitive, imaginative, introspective, deep thinking, philosophical, artistic, intelligent, compassionate, perfectionist.

WEAKNESSES

Withdrawn, reclusive, stays in shell, critical, elusive, loner, devious, timid, escapist tendencies, repressed emotions, secretive, like their own way, sarcastic, cunning.

LIFE PATH EIGHT

The number eight itself is very like the symbol of infinity. 8. It's a number of perfect balance. Turn it any way and it remains true. You can turn it upside down, back to front or reflect it in a mirror and it still looks exactly the same. This is the real truth behind the number 8. It is said that this is the life path where the soul is seeking to learn to deal with the physical universe but this life path is much, much deeper than that. In fact it is a very scorpionic life path. It's no coincidence that Scorpio is the eighth sign of the zodiac. These souls are deep and powerful and can be quite a force to be reckoned with.

The soul choosing to experience life on the eight life path will usually have had a previous life of either extreme excess or extreme deprivation. This could be the soul who has starved to death through their inability to manifest the resources necessary to sustain life. It can also be the soul who has recently experienced a life of incredible abundance, taking far more than their fair share of the earth's resources. Through owning and keeping too many material possessions or conversely living without the material objects it needed, the soul needs to learn how to balance their needs with their wants. In the reflection period between lives, the soul will have recognised the imbalance they have experienced and will be seeking to address this by choosing the eight life path.

An eight who is on track will be in a position of responsibility. They have great organisational skills and loads of energy. They can become very wealthy and successful but the lesson is to be satisfied with achieving material success and then to open their hearts to share their material resources with others. Once in balance, the eight can enjoy the material universe and the comfort of nice things.

There is a danger that the shadow of the previous life, the life just before this incarnation, is too heavy to shake off. For the soul who has had a life of insufficiency, then this can manifest as the hoarder, the person who can't bear to throw stuff away and who hangs on to physical possessions that they no longer need. There can also be a strong desire for possessions, the 'must have' feeling. The eights then become the consumers of the world. They consume objects, food or money. For these souls the question that needs to be uppermost in their mind when they seek to acquire is 'Do I need this or do I just desire this?' They also need to learn not to come from fear.

For the soul who has had more than enough resources in the last life (or too many possessions), they might go completely the opposite way in this life and choose to have nothing so that they don't feel encumbered by possessions. Sometimes, however, they find it difficult to live with less than they were accustomed to in their previous life. They arrive on earth and want whatever they desire. This desire needs to be tempered.

Either way, possessions and belongings are an issue with this life path. Most progress can be made on this life path if the soul can reach the stage whereby they have enough to live on and choose to give the surplus money/food/belongings to those in greater need. An example would be a successful business person who chooses to give all income over a certain amount each year to a charity. Or a working person who donates 10% of their income to a soup kitchen for the homeless.

Attaining money, status and power is not the final goal of an eight. The goal is the satisfaction of becoming materially self sufficient and using their power in a compassionate and caring way.

RELATIONSHIPS

If you are in a relationship with an eight then be prepared for an expensive ride. Eights like shopping and eating out. They are usually interested in clothes, gadgets, good food and nice cars. They enjoy what the world has to offer in the material realm and that comes at a price. They like to spend and can easily get themselves into debt, so make sure you can afford life with an eight before you get too involved. Their stubbornness can be a problem but they're fun and energetic so they make stimulating partners.

THE EIGHT CHILD

If you are raising an eight child then it would be a good idea to put them in situations where they can see for themselves the unequal distribution of wealth in the world. Sponsoring a child in a third world country would give them the opportunity to grow up with the awareness that too few people hold too much of the wealth. Or maybe they could be encouraged to donate their unwanted toys to charity on a regular basis. "There are children in the world who have no toys to play with. Would you like to choose some of your toys to give to these children?"

Teach them early to ask themselves 'Do I need to buy this or do I just desire this?'

DESTINY NUMBER EIGHT

STRENGTHS

Powerful, can become famous, perceptive, ambitious, successful, leadership qualities, reliable, humanitarian, wise.

WEAKNESSES

Hunger for power, too interested in money, self centred and vain, intolerant of others, stubborn, greedy, grasping, controlling, misuse of power.

LIFE PATH NINE

Nine is the highest of the single digits. Nine is a life of tying up loose ends. It's very difficult for a nine to be constant in this life.

The soul who wants to turn over a new leaf will often choose to incarnate on this life path. This is the soul who has come to the realisation that they are on a journey and at some point they will need to return to the source. At a soul level they have recognised that they are a droplet from the ocean and that their destination is the ocean itself. (Of course I don't mean LITERALLY but that they recognise their connection to Life with a capital 'L'). They are not necessarily aware of this consciously. We are all connected, all aspects of the one consciousness. What I do, think and say affects the world. And so it is with all of us. We are not isolated units of consciousness. The soul on the nine life path has chosen to move their soul onwards towards acting upon this realisation. The main lesson of the nine is to learn to give purely for the satisfaction of helping others and not giving in order to be rewarded. This is how a spiritually advanced being acts, offering their life in service to others and giving selflessly.

In the reflection period between lives this soul will have chosen to over view more than just the life immediately preceding this life. They will have identified a pattern of selfishness running like a thread through their lifetimes. Now they are ready to deal with that aspect of themselves and open themselves up to the idea of losing their ego. They want to change and they are trying to do that by choosing the nine life path. In moving away from selfishness they need to learn to think of the needs and feelings of other people. In this life they are learning to give to others. They can find themselves placed in situations where they have little choice but to give, such as being nursemaid to a sick child or carer for an elderly relative. The key lesson is to surrender to their situation and give with selfless love.

The day to day life of a nine can be fragmented. Relationships can be short as partners can find the intensity of the emotions of a nine difficult to handle. They are often on the move or can live in different places in their lives. What they are doing is coming into contact with people and situations that can give them the opportunity to be of service. Relationships that have been left unresolved, aspects of soul development that have not been pursued to a natural conclusion, abilities that have never born fruit and negative traits that need erasing are all areas that the nine may chose to work on in this life.

A nine who is on track will be involved in charity work, caring for the sick, needy or under privileged. Their giving might be in the form of friendship or love towards others. They will be giving for the sake of giving and not for any reward or return.

Unfortunately a negative nine is quite common. A nine who is off track will still be displaying a marked degree of selfishness and self-centredness in this life. If you are a nine who is pursuing personal goals for personal gain, then you would be wise to re-assess your life direction, for the key to success on this particular life path is to give up the idea of needing personal satisfaction and rewards for what you do. To help others selflessly requires practical work. It's no good having the idea of helping if you do nothing about it.

Once on track and surrendered to giving, this life path brings huge rewards at the level of the soul.

RELATIONSHIPS

If you are in a relationship with a nine, understanding their life path will help to give you the patience that you will need to deal with them at an everyday level. They're not the easiest of partners to live with as they have high standards. They are always looking for the 'perfect' relationship. Nines love with depth and intensity and if they do not receive the same level of emotion from their partner, the relationship can fail and the nine will pursue the deep emotional bond that they crave elsewhere.

THE NINE CHILD

If you are raising a nine child then allow them the opportunity to do something creative as an outlet for their emotional nature. Art or drama classes, learning a musical instrument or expressive dance are ways for the nine to express themselves and will act as a release valve for their feelings. Be guided by your child. They will often intuitively know where they need to be and what they need to learn. Teach them to set goals such as achieving grade one in piano or reaching blue belt in karate. Once they have achieved their goal then help them to decide whether they want to continue in each activity and set a new goal, or whether they want to drop that particular activity and try something new.

Because at a soul level this child is learning to think of others, having a pet to look after and care for would be a good way to help the child to develop unselfishness. To care for another, whether it is an animal or a human, will teach the child the skills needed to take the emphasis away from self.

DESTINY NUMBER NINE

STRENGTHS
Philosophical, intelligent, sincere, wise, generous, adventurous, sensitive, sophisticated, kind and compassionate, wise, evolved, giving, charitable, can be highly artistic and creative, tolerant, broad minded.

WEAKNESSES
Over emotional, self-pitying, moody, critical, can be resentful about giving, too emotional, argumentative, selfish, 'the dreamer', tight fisted.

CHAPTER SIX

THE MASTER LIFE PATHS

Being on a master number life path does not automatically mean that you are a master of something. Any life path number expressing at its highest potential can produce masters. However, the heightened energy of a master life path gives you the potential of being a catalyst for change in the world.

MASTER LIFE PATH ELEVEN

The number 11 is a master number. Here we have the first life path that is not a single digit. Not only that, eleven is both a prime number and a binary number. Even the 22 life path, although generally considered the most powerful life path, cannot claim to be a prime number. Nor is 22 a binary number. So the eleven life path is quite unique.

I always refer to those souls on an eleven life path as 'eleveners'. There is always something slightly different about these souls and it's almost impossible to identify just what that 'je ne sais quoi' is. You can find elevens in all walks of life. They can be found running the country or living rough on the street. Yet wherever they are found and whoever they are, in my experience there's almost always a mystique about these people.

What makes a soul choose the eleven life path? It's because now that soul has chosen to experience being in the physical universe whilst carrying a vibration than can be used for the good of others. All numbers carry a vibration. The 11 (a compound number) carries a much higher vibration than the single digits. Being an elevener is a bit like having a VIP pass that will get you into places that most of us can't get into. These souls, though their actions in prior incarnations, have decided that they are ready to take their place on earth and be of use in some way.

If you check out the numbers and identify any eleveners amongst your friends and family, you might question this statement. You might find the elevener who does not appear to be making any mark on the world and who seemingly is living a very ordinary life. That's because, having incarnated with their VIP pass, they realise that bringing this vibration into the earth plane of physical reality is not quite as easy as it might have appeared from the astral plane.

When we are on the astral plane, there is a lightness of being, and time is not like it is here on earth. Grandiose plans that appear perfectly possible to manifest from that level of consciousness are suddenly experienced as very difficult here on the earthly plane. It's a bit like the difference between walking through air and walking through mud. Things are much slower, heavier and more cumbersome here on the earth than there on the astral.

The soul on an eleven life path is charged with energy. This energy is held in the nervous system. Too much of this energy buzzing through them can cause the eleven to be very highly strung.

The main danger of an eleven is slipping into lethargy and giving up on their soul's impulse to be a force of good. Being here in the world can all get too much, too dispiriting and depressing and so the eleven can either fall into a comfortable rut or into a very negative state of mind. There will be times in the life of an eleven when the soul stirs and the possibility for change is presented, but it is up to the soul to seize that opportunity.

RELATIONSHIPS

If you are in a relationship with an eleven you need to be aware that they are energetically charged with an over active nervous system. Stress can make them rather difficult to live with as it'll be their nearest and dearest who will be on the receiving end of any inability to keep calm and balanced. Bear in mind that your partner needs to fulfil their soul journey so try and be supportive of them if they suddenly decide to do something radical, like opening a free school or going to Africa to volunteer in a refugee camp.

THE ELEVEN CHILD

If you are responsible for a child who is on an eleven life path, you need to remind yourself that you are dealing with a soul who is carrying a heightened amount of nervous energy. The eleven is not an average child. Try and provide a calm space for the child on a regular basis. I know that might not be easy if you have a lively household and twenty other children, but giving the eleven child access to calming music such as a recording of dolphins swimming in the sea can be an effective way of soothing the child's soul. I'd especially recommend this at bedtime so they are eased gently into sleep. The sooner the eleven child can learn to self-relax, the better he/she will be able to cope with their sensitive nervous system. Try and find a children's yoga class where they will be taught postures and exercises that will help to keep their nervous system in balance. Singing is great therapy for an eleven. Have some CD's in the car and make singing part of your car journeys. Controlling their breath through singing will help to keep their nervous systems in good health.

DESTINY NUMBER ELEVEN

STRENGTHS

Working for the common good, spiritual, powerful, a leader, brave, inventive, intuitive, psychic, big visions, high ideals, deep thinking, creative, inspiring.

WEAKNESSES

Nervous problems, indecision, fearful, insecure, inhibited, inferiority complex, over sensitive, daydreamer, opinionated, addiction issues.

MASTER LIFE PATH TWENTY TWO

Number twenty two is the eleventh life path that the soul might choose. This is considered the most powerful of all the life paths. It is also the rarest one. As stated earlier in the book, there are eleven life paths; 1-9, 11 and 22.

Eleven and twenty two are the master life paths and with them come extra responsibilities. I personally hold the number eleven as superior to the number twenty two and my understanding is that the number twenty two is shorthand for a double eleven, 11:11. The twenty two life path could therefore be referred to as the 11:11 path, the ultimate life path at this point of time in the evolution of the earth.

Are you a twenty two? What are you doing with your life? How are you contributing to the betterment of this world? What are you doing for others? These are some of the questions that need to be asked by the soul on a twenty two life path.

To choose a twenty two life path is a huge responsibility. Here is the soul with the potential to be a force for change in the world. In the reflection period between lives huge realisations will have taken place. A lot of progress will have been made on the spiritual path in previous lives. Often the twenty two does not have to be reborn but chooses to come back to the earthly plane to help others. The trouble is, although the vision of what the twenty two might be able to create on earth looks very clear on the astral plane, things are not quite so clear when the soul finds itself encased in the heavy physical body and living in the physical realm. On the astral plane the twenty two will have been filled with enthusiasm and confidence, eager to move forward and make a difference on our planet, maybe, for example, by introducing new concepts, creating art that breaks boundaries, teaching mind-opening techniques or manifesting ground breaking discoveries. But, rather like the eleven life path, when the weight of the physical becomes too much for this soul, they can feel over burdened and weighed down. In turn this means that they usually don't live up to their potential. In fact they rarely do. They then have a tendency to become despondent and depressed.

The nervous system of a twenty has a huge amount of nervous energy running through it, even more than that of an eleven. Rather like a wire with too much electrical current running through it, a twenty two can easily blow a fuse and consequently they can suffer from nervous disorders.

More than anything, the twenty two needs to rediscover their clarity of purpose here on earth. They will have experienced clarity whilst on the astral plane. It is very rare indeed to find a twenty two who has managed to keep their focus on their goal once they are in the physical body. A foggy mind, a sluggish body and weary heart tend to be the manifestation of a twenty two who has lost their way.

There are ways to work towards overcoming this tendency. Meditation is great for clearing the mind and re-connecting with the 'between lives' clarity. Sitting with eyes closed and the internal gaze on the third eye (situated on the forehead just above the space in between the eyebrows) allows the connection between the physical self and the higher self to clear. Just spending a few minutes each day doing this will help, but I'd also suggest annual retreats where the soul can withdraw from everyday life for eleven days. The retreat can be formal or informal. Eleven days fishing, for example, could be just as beneficial as eleven days in a monastery. Twenty twos just need to spend time away from other people, away from family, normal day to day life, work and the home. These retreats from the outer world need to be spent completely alone, not with friends, partner or family in tow. Pay attention to diet during the retreat. Try to eat pure, unprocessed food and cut out alcohol and smoking. Twenty two's sometimes smoke. The reason for this is that the smoke acts as a protection and they look through the world through the soft haze of a smoke filled aura. That's easier on their nervous system than being completely open and vulnerable. By choosing to smoke the twenty two is going off track and is not being true to the urge of the soul. There are better ways to build protection. Yoga breathing exercises and movements that build chi such as Chi Gong are more effective and safer than smoking.

If you are a twenty two (11:11), don't waste this opportunity to share your gifts and talents with the world. Remind yourself that you are here for the benefit of humankind. Be gentle with yourself, pray for help and support and try and stay positive.

RELATIONSHIPS

More than any other number, the twenty two is deeply affected by their early life experiences. Unless they have consciously worked towards healing their inner child, they will bring their issues into their adult relationships. If you are with an unhealed twenty two then the relationship can be beset with problems. If you are with a healed twenty two then you will have an inspiring and steady partner of great depth

THE TWENTY TWO CHILD

If you are the parent of a soul that has chosen a twenty two life path, you have a very important job to do. The early years are very important, in particular the first twelve months of life. You are raising a soul of high vibration. Try to keep the child near you as much as possible during the first year. If you do not respond to the cries of a twenty two baby you could weaken their connection to the earth. Their nervous system is so sensitive it is easily damaged.

DESTINY NUMBER TWENTY TWO

STRENGTHS
Common sense, intuition, charisma, leadership ability, able to think out of the box, able to manifest ideas, powerful, commanding, grounded.

WEAKNESSES
Aloof, withdrawn, inflexible, stubborn, nervous, controlling and manipulative, arrogant.

CHAPTER SEVEN

REPEATED DIGITS

Numbers are cosmic consciousness breaking through into your ego-centred world. When a repeated digit appears to you, it's simply the energy of that particular number manifesting itself in an intensified way. Pure energy, in the form of a number, is asking you to take note of what it is saying. It's trying to get a message through to you. It's very simple. 111 is the energy of the number one coming in strongly, 222 is the energy of the number two coming in strongly, 333 is the energy of the number three coming in strongly and so on.

However, it takes practice to learn how to interpret the message of each number. Sometimes the numbers could just be telling you that the situation you are in has the energy of that particular number. Or if a repeated digit appears around a person then that person is carrying the energy of that particular number.

However, the key to interpreting repeated digits is to interpret them in conjunction with the time and place that they choose to appear to you. **They cannot be interpreted out of context.** Think of the numbers as a messenger, the interface between your seen and your unseen worlds.

When a number prompt appears to you, take note of the following:

What (or who) were you thinking about at that moment?

Who were you with?

Where were you?

What could you see in your immediate environment?

Where were you going in that moment?

What were you doing?

There are times when a number sequence appears in my everyday life very strongly yet I can't read the message it is bringing. I simply can't find the message. That doesn't mean the message isn't there. I have a very close relationship with numbers but our communication is not perfect. However, there are times when I am completely blown away by the way that numbers get their message across and that is why I take so much notice of them.

Numbers might be screaming a message at you but if you're not in full awareness in each moment, you will miss the appearance of the number and the message will not be received. Living with awareness will help you to relate to the world of number. I don't follow numbers blindly. Even if a hundred numbers appear to me with a message, if something doesn't feel right I won't do it. I always listen to my intuition before I act. The following interpretations of number signs are based on my own experience and indicate how I use numbers to guide me. I find number patterns work best as prompts. When I have already had the feeling that I need to do something, a number prompt acts like a nudge in my ribs, telling me that I was right and to get on and do it. As such, they are a confirmation sign.

When you see a repeated number sign, try to remember that:

1 is about beginnings and starting things

2 is about relationship, choice and duality

3 is about past, present and future and moving forward

4 is about structure, safety and security

5 is about change, instability, travel and communication

6 is about peace, balance, harmony and beauty

7 is about spirituality and introspection

8 is about worldly success and the material universe

9 is about finishing off, tying up loose ends and gaining wisdom

0 is about linking, wiping the slate clean or returning to nothingness

The following interpretations of repeated numbers are only for your guidance. It is up to you to find your own personal interpretations. Only YOU are living your life and only YOU can read your world.

1 1 1

1 is about new beginnings. When it shows itself in repeated form in your everyday life, you're being reminded that you have an opportunity to start something new. It's prompting you, giving you a nudge that says "come on, get started, move on, stop procrastinating!"

> *I had enquired online about a yoga course. For some reason they accidently replied to my email five times - all sent at exactly 11:11! I took that as a sign that I needed to do the course. Later that same day I was in a queue of traffic and the registration number of the car in front contained the letters initials YO (Yoga) and the number 11. I did the course.*

222

2 is about relationship. 222 is often linked to somebody who you have had a relationship with but who has now died. They are watching over you from the astral plane. There are many souls who have chosen to be on the astral plane during the earth shifts of 2012, which is when the cosmic computer re-boots, a time of mass awakening and the arrival of the Age of Aquarius. We're still on the cusp of Pisces and Aquarius but after 21.12.2012 then we'll no longer be on the cusp. We will have moved fully into Aquarius. (Look how many 2's are in that date.) So when you see the 222, know that someone is guiding you. They're trying to get a message through to you. They need you to take note of what is around you so that you can read their message.

I was sitting in the car, stuck in traffic (always a good time to look for signs!) and I noticed that it was 2.22pm on my digital clock. My trip meter was reading 22.2. I realised that someone was sending me a message. I looked around. Where was the message? I was stuck behind a refuse lorry and when I looked closely I saw the word SMILE written by somebody's finger in the dust on this dirty vehicle. There it was! I was going through a difficult time and I had been in tears earlier that day so I was being reminded to stay positive. I thought this was such a clever way to get the message through. I just love the magic of the language of numbers.

333

3 is about timing, about past, present and future. This is a very spiritual and magical number. The message it carries is to ask you to move something on. Don't be stuck in the past or project too far into the future. This is a power number and it's reminding you to use your power in a way that will make a difference in the world. You have personal power and it's your will that decides in which direction this power will be directed. The clue to the message that the 333 is carrying will be where this number appears.

I had been thinking about visiting a sacred site in India. It was in a remote location and difficult to reach. I was online looking for hotels in the area I wanted to visit and I managed to find one. There was nothing stopping me from going. I then noticed the time was exactly 3.33. I knew this was a prompt to get me to book my trip. I have taken note of that prompt and I'm seriously considering booking.

(Whilst writing these very words I noticed that the time was exactly 13.33. I was being reminded yet again that I need to book this trip.....!)

444

444 is a safety net. It's about security. The number 4 is associated with the square and when the number appears in sequence then you can relax and know that you are safe. It's the sign of reassurance. Maybe you've been worrying about paying a bill or being evicted from the safety and comfort of your home. The 444 is asking you not to worry, for whatever happens you're on the right path and even if your situation seems difficult, is the perfect thing for you at this point in time. You are being asked to accept your situation and trust the Universe.

It was snowing outside when my gas boiler broke down. I had no heating or hot water. It was a Sunday so I thought I would have to leave my home and go and stay with a friend. I looked for the boiler insurance policy details and the customer service number I had to call began 08444. Seeing that 444 reminded me that everything was unfolding perfectly and I need not worry. The phone helpline was open 24 hours, 7 days a week. My boiler was fixed later that day.

555

Three fives in a sequence can have quite a few different meanings. Isn't that just typical of the changeable number five? Remember, 5 is about change, instability travel and communication. Are you being asked to change something in your life, share some gift you have, break free of something or seize an opportunity that has been presented to you? The next time the 555 appears to you, at that very moment look around for clues. Where are you when you see the 555?

I was thinking of taking a trip up to Rosslyn Castle in Scotland. I went online to find out the cost of a rail ticket to Edinburgh. I saw that the train was timetabled to arrive at 5.55pm. That small number prompt was all I needed to confirm what I was feeling I needed to do. I decided to break free from home for a few days and visit the castle. I had an amazing time and I was so pleased that 555 had given me the 'nudge'.

666

This is the number of perfection. Most people think it's a bad or evil number but it's not (SEE END OF THIS CHAPTER). It's strongly linked to beauty and relationships. When the 666 appears in front of you, just think of the key words 'perfection, beauty, harmony, relationship'. Then look around you for the message.

My friend went to a see a flat on the High street. It was number 666 so she didn't want to live there because she had grown up with the idea that 666 was evil. The garden was a complete mess and it backed onto the railway station. But at least it had a garden and the flat was cheap and convenient for local transport so she took it. Gradually she cleared the garden. She planted flowers and put out food for the birds. Soon it was a colourful oasis in the concrete jungle. What's more, it could be seen from the platform of the railway station, brightening the lives of the commuters as they stood on the platform waiting for the train. Here was the 666 bringing beauty to lots of people, even though Lynne's decision to rent the flat was not a conscious response to the number 666.

777

Classically the number 7 has the reputation as a very lucky number. It is also recognised as a spiritual number. When the 777 appears you are being reminded of the spiritual aspect of yourself. *(Remember, the key words are spirituality and introspection.)* Often it's an opportunity being presented. Do you have the courage to accept?

I was on my way to meet someone. It was our first meeting. As I drew up outside his house, the last 3 digits of the milometer in the car displayed exactly 777. I knew that was a good sign. This person became a very good friend and he helped me enormously on my spiritual path. In particular, he taught me to be in the moment.

888

888 is a very material number and it's linked with status and position in the world. If the 888 appears around a certain person, that person could be very helpful to you in your career. If it appears within a relationship (maybe your partner was born in August 1988 or lives at number 88 in the street, or their phone number contains the 888) then this relationship could be very successful and your partner could be beneficial to you.

I was having problems with my knee. Not far from my home was a Chinese medical centre. It was in shop number 888. That's probably why the owner bought the shop in the first place as the Chinese believe 8 to be a very fortunate number. The owner of the shop was an amazing acupuncturist and herbalist who healed my knee.

999

999 is the emergency number for the police, fire or ambulance in some countries so in the mass consciousness it is usually associated with danger or an emergency of some kind. However, the appearance of the 999 is not a warning sign. It's simply asking

you to bring something to completion. This might be a project that you started but didn't finish. It could be a relationship that needs to come to a resolution. The 999 is an important sign to listen to because it's telling you that you need to complete something in order to move on. If you don't heed it you could get stuck and looking back on your life you'll realise that you wasted time.

James had worked in a call centre for several years. He'd taken the job to raise some money so that he could afford to go to travelling. At work he noticed that the number 999 was appearing so frequently that he asked me what it meant for him. I suggested he was being told that the time had come to give up the job at the call centre and travel. He took my advice and now he is somewhere in India.

000

It's quite rare for the 000 or 0000 to appear without any other numbers and when it does, it's acting like a full stop. It's the universe saying to you that something has come to an end. It has come 'full circle'. That can be viewed as either positive or negative, depending on how you choose to look at it.

Some people think that zero means nothing. Nobody is born on a pure zero day, month or year as they don't exist. Those born in the year 2000 have the 3 zeros in their birth date but the 2 in 2000 overrides those 3 zeros. In our everyday life the 000 does have meaning.

Janet had been in an abusive relationship for months but was too afraid to leave her violent partner. One evening she was heating up a meal in the microwave and the timer jammed. It simply wouldn't register any number other than 00.00. It still worked and heated the food but that 00.00 would not go away. She knew it meant something. That night she had an almighty row with her partner.

She was deeply unhappy. In the morning when she heated up the milk for her coffee the 00.00 was still there on the microwave. Then she realised what it meant. Her relationship was over, it was time to leave.

NUMBER PATTERNS

As previously stated in this book, numbers are simply an energy manifesting in the form of a numeral. Patterns such as 1212, 20102012, 1331, 30003 and 55155 are therefore energy in a pattern. They appear in a pattern so that they can grab your attention. Let's face it, you are more likely to notice the number 11 22 33 than 212313. Same numbers, same amount of times, different order, that's all. So the numbers appear as patterns to get their message through to you.

A repeated digit within the year of birth is significant. The only days of the month that contain the same repeated digit are the 11th and the 22nd. It just so happens that these are the two master numbers. The only month with a repeated double digit is November, the 11th month, again a master number. When two repeated digits are next to each other, their strength is more than doubled. When there are three digits together then that number is much more powerful. A person born on 5th may 1955 (5/5/1955) is actually on a 3 life path but in this instance, with the 5 being repeated 4 times, then the influence of the number 5 life path would be very apparent in the person.

However, you can have repeated digits within a date of birth that are not next to each other. This does lessen their effect but can still be considered as having an influence. The 19th January 1989 (19/1/1989 OR 1/19/1989) has three 1's and three 9's which strengthens the 1 and 9 vibration within the life path.

Here's an example:

19/08/1988

This date has two 1's, two 9's and three 8's. The life path for this soul is

1+9=10=**1**. 0+8=**8**. 1+9+8+8=26=**8**. **1+8+8=17=8**

Look how often the 8 appears! This is a soul with a very heavy emphasis on the 8 life path. However, as the 1's and 9's are also repeated, this soul can read the 1 and 9 life path to reveal underlying influences in their life's direction.

DAYS AND DATES

Dates such as 11.11.2011 or 22.2.2012 can be interpreted in the same way as a date of birth. Look at the date 11.11.2011. 11 is a master number so it's not reduced to a single digit. 11=**11**. 11=**11**. 2+0+11=13=**4**. **11+11+4=26=8**, so the energy of that day is the energy of 8.

What about 21.12.2012 (12.21.2012) which is the famous date of the ending of the Mayan calendar?

2+1=**3**. 1+2=**3**. 2+0+1+2=**5**. 3+3+5=**11**. **11** is not reduced so it's not surprising that this very significant date is a master number day.

You can use this calculation to discover the number energy of any given day.

Is 666 an evil number?

There is a widely held belief that the number 666 is the number of the devil. This belief probably originates from the following verse from the book of revelations in the bible.

Here is wisdom. Let him that hath understanding count the number of the beast: for it is the number of a man; and his number is 666.
REVELATIONS 13:18

Man is not just a physical being. He is a Trinity. He has a body, soul and spirit. He functions on 3 planes of being; the physical, the astral and the spiritual. In esoteric numerology the numbers 3, 6 and 9 relate to the spiritual plane, 2, 5 and 8 to the astral plane and 1, 4 and 7 to the physical plane. Arranged as below, each vertical column adds up to 6.

3	6	9	Spiritual
2	5	8	Astral
1	4	7	Physical
Total: 6	Total: 15 =6	Total: 24 =6	

When perfected man is fully developed in body (physical), mind (astral) and spirit then his numbers do indeed add up to 666.

666, to him who hath understanding is the number of perfected man.

- *Add up the numbers 1-36 (1+2+3+4+5etc) and they add up to....666!*

CHAPTER EIGHT

NUMBER 23

According to Wikipedia, the **23 enigma** refers to the belief that most incidents and events are directly connected to the number 23, some modification of the number 23, or a number related to the number 23.

Not very long ago a film called 'The Number 23' appeared in cinemas worldwide. It was a frightening film, based on the appearance of the number 23 in the life of a young man. This number had begun to appear to him in his everyday life not long after he had bought a book about the number 23 in a second-hand bookshop. However, the film was fictional.

A German film simply called '23' is a 1998 film about a young hacker who apparently committed suicide on May 23, 1989. The young man who died had an obsession with the number 23. This film was based on real life events. Following controversy over the content of the film, the director, Hans-Christian Schmidt, subsequently co-authored a book that told the story of the making of 23 and also detailed the differences between the film and the actual events.

The film 'A Beautiful Mind' was based on the life of the renowned American mathematician John Forbes Nash who was a Nobel Prize-winning economist. He was obsessed with the number 23. This number was a prominent feature in his battle with mental illness. His breakdown began when he claimed that a photograph of Pope John XXIII on the cover of Life magazine held a secret message for him, the proof being that 23 was his favourite prime number.

The number 23 holds a special place in the lives of many people. Like the time prompt 11:11, 23 is a number with a huge following. Google '23 enigma' and millions of pages will come up. Why is the number 23 held in such high esteem? Is there anything special or different about the number 23? Is the mystery surrounding the number 23 fact, fiction or random?

The 23 phenomenon does exist. I know, because I experienced it.

Some years ago I had a car accident. It was a very upsetting incident as it involved a young child. Shortly after the accident I went on holiday to the island of Ibiza with a friend. There I met a man who told me that the number was 23. I had not asked him a question. He just gave me that information out of the blue. 'What do you mean, the number is 23?' I asked, but he would say no more on the subject. He simply repeated that the number was 23 and suggested that I read a trilogy of books called 'The Illuminatus Trilogy'. I assumed he was either completely mad or high on drugs.

Arriving back at work the following week at the school where I was teaching, I was approached by the headmistress who was carrying a huge envelope. She handed it to me. All that was written on the envelope was a massive number 23. I was shocked and I asked her why she had written that. She explained that our school was number 23 on the internal mail system and that all our mail was marked with the number 23. Feeling worried, I went up to my classroom and looked down the list of teachers on my pin board. I was teacher number 23. I looked back in my diary to discover the date of my car accident. It had happened on 23rd June. I added up the number of my bank account. 23. My passport number. 23. My birth date. 23. Everything in my life added up to 23.

W is the 23rd letter of the alphabet. I was living in Walthamstow, London, starting AND ending with the letter W. My post code added up to 23. In fact everything in my life was connected to either the number 23 or the reversed number 32. What was strange was the fact that these 23s had existed in my life BEFORE I went to Ibiza but I had not noticed them until my encounter with the strange man on holiday. Apophenia is the experience of seeing meaningful patterns or connections in random or meaningless data, but there is no way that the overpowering way in which the 23 appeared to me at that time could be called meaningless. It was, quite literally, connected to everything in my life.

I was scared. I didn't know what it all meant. This was happening in the days before the internet so I couldn't just google it and connect with other people on the planet who were experiencing it. I had nowhere to turn for help or guidance.

I bought the Illuminatus Trilogy by Robert Anton Wilson and Robert O'Shea. These three books link the number 23 with a self styled religion called Discordia. Just a few pages into the first book I read the following sentence:

'And I tell you this, never trust anyone with the initials H.C.'

My name is Hilary Carter. Now I was beginning to panic! Looking back, that was the day that everything in my life came tumbling down. What I was experiencing was way beyond coincidence. I could no longer look at the Universe in the same way. It was as if I was a computer and I had crashed. The reference to the initials H.C. on top of all those 23s was one coincidence too many for my mind to handle. This was tipping point. In order not to fall over the edge, I had to clear out of my mind everything I had ever learned. In other words, I had to wipe my hard drive clean. I was either going to have a breakdown or a breakthrough.

So does the 23 have a meaning? Is it, as mystics through the centuries have claimed, an important and significant number?

I have no doubt that 23 is an exceptional number in human affairs. In the I Ching, the Chinese 'Book of Change' there are 64 hexagrams. Hexagram 23 is 'complete breakdown'. That's the message of 23 in a nutshell. When the 23 appears in every part of your life it's your personal hard drive being wiped. It's your cosmic alarm clock going off, telling you that it's time to wake up from this dream that we call reality. It can be a rude awakening. 23 is not subtle.

Many people are raised with the belief that we are born, we die, and then we either go to heaven or hell. When the number 23 enters your life in a major way then your breakthrough has arrived. At the level of the soul, it's a success story because you have managed to bring your astral consciousness onto the earth plane. 23 represents the lifting of the veil between the astral and the physical and can be followed by the re-emergence of past life remembrance. I could easily have had a breakdown when my 23 alarm went off. Fortunately for me, a friend turned up on my doorstep just as I was struggling with the appearance of the H.C. Her down to earth manner and total lack of interest in my coincidences helped to keep me sane. (Thank you for being there at that moment, Lynne...).

Breakdown can also be called breakthrough. Like the phoenix arising from the ashes, your mind needs to be completely freed from its programming before the new consciousness can replace the old. Of course 23 is followed by the number 24 which is the number of renewal so number 23 need not be feared as it will be followed by a renewal of many things in your life.

I doubt that all beings will need to go through the 23 process to break through into the raised consciousness of the Age of Aquarius, but a core number of us will need to.

MAGIC SQUARE OF 15

The compound numbers of 23 or the reversed 32 both add up to 5. If we take the numerals 1-9 and arrange them into a magic square, then all the columns (vertical/horizontal/diagonal) add up to 15. There are other magic squares but the magic square of 15 is the most important in that it is the only one in which the numerals 1-9 appear only once. 5 is the central number of this square. This is what makes the 5 such a special number. It is the

ONLY number that is in contact with all the others.

8	1	6
3	5	7
4	9	2

Is this the secret of the 23? It is the breakdown of 5 into a prime number, the lowest prime number with 2 consecutive digits and it signifies that we have reached the central core of the magic square. That is the way out of this illusion, bound by the confines of time, hence the expression '23 skidoo' which means 'let's get out of here'.

5 is recognised as the number of freedom but 23 is the number of greater freedom, freedom from the 'programme' that most humans are currently trapped in. Some people call that the matrix.

What I find particularly interesting about the magic square is that the number 15, when written as a binary number, is 1111. That brings us to the curiosity of the 11:11 phenomenon. (see next chapter).

FACTS ABOUT THE NUMBER 23

- 23 has been the subject of three films to date:
  1. The 1999 German movie called 23, about a young hacker called Karl Koch. (Note his initials KK. K is the 11th letter of the alphabet; read about 11:11 in the next chapter.)
  . 2. The Number 23, starring Jim Carrey
  3. A Beautiful Mind starring Russell Crowe

- Mathematician John Nash, subject of the film 'A Beautiful Mind' published 23 scientific articles.

- The most detailed account of the assassination of Julius Caesar, written by Nicolaus of Damascus, claims numerous enemies stabbed the Roman emperor 23 times. The wounds ranged from superficial to mortal.

- The Knights Templar had 23 Grand Masters.

- William Shakespeare was born in Stratford Upon Avon on 23 April 1564. He died 52 years later on his birthday, 23 April 1616.

- In the television series Lost, one of the six numbers that haunt the characters and which they have to input to a computer to avoid an unknown fate is 23.

- The Birthday Paradox states that a group of 23 randomly-selected people is the smallest number where there will be a probability higher than 50 per cent that two people will share the same birthday.

- Whilst living in Tangiers, the author William Burroughs met a ferryman called Captain Clark. Clark told Burroughs that his ferry had been crossing from Tangiers to Spain for 23 years without incident. That same day the ferry sank and Clark died. Whilst digesting that information, a radio bulletin announced the crash of Flight number 23 on the New York-Miami route. The pilot was called Captain Clark. It is said that from then on Burroughs was obsessed with the number 23.

- The twin towers attack on 11 September 2001 was a 23 day. (Remember, the 11 is a master number so it is not reduced down) so (11+9+2+0+0+1) add up to 23.

- Discordianism, a religion based on the premise that discord and chaos are the building blocks of life, reveres 23 as a sacred number. 23 is the number attributed to the goddess Eris, who surveys a world of chaos.

- Michael Jordan, the American basketball player and footballer David Beckham both wore the shirt number 23.

- In 2003 Manchester City director Dennis Tueart confirmed that the club would retire the number 23 shirt as a mark of respect to midfielder Marc-Vivien Foe who died after collapsing on the pitch wearing the number 23. (BBC Sport 27/6/2003)

- Ask anybody to name a psalm and the chances are that they will name psalm 23. It is the most well known psalm. "The Lord is my shepherd; I shall not want. He maketh me to lie down in green pastures: He leadeth me beside the still waters."

- Each parent contributes 23 chromosomes to the human embryo. The nuclei of cells in human bodies have 46 chromosomes made out of 23 pairs. Egg and sperm cells in humans have 23 chromosomes which fuse and divide to create an embryo.

- The first ever American morse code transmission was- "What hath God wrought?" It was from the Bible passage Numbers 23:23.

- "23 skidoo" is an American catchphrase from the early 20th century. It means 'let's get out of here'.

- 2 divided by 3 is 666 recurring.

- The Titanic sank on 15.4.1912. 1+5+4+1+9+1+2=23

- The earth is tilted at 23.5 degrees.

- The Romans used 23 letters to write Latin:
  A B C D E F G H I K L M N O P Q R S T V X Y Z

- In Aleister Crowley's *Cabalistic Dictionary*, he defines the number 23 as the number of "parting, removal, separation, joy, a thread, and life..."

- Computers: World Wide Web=WWW. W is the 23rd letter of the alphabet.

- In The Matrix Reloaded, Neo is told it is important to choose 23 people to *repopulate Zion.*

- 23 is part of the Fibonacci series of numbers

- The most common name for popes is John, having occurred 23 times.

- Mercury, the nearest planet to our sun, is never more than 23 degrees from the sun

- It is claimed that 23 Annunuki seeded life on this planet

- 23 is the first prime number in which both digits are prime numbers and add up to another prime number.

- Comedian Tony Hancock lived at 23 Railway Cuttings

- The 23rd tarot card is the hanged Man.

- In the film 'Jeepers Creepers' the demon known as 'The Creeper' appears every 23rd spring for 23 days to feast on human beings.

- The flashbacks in the film 'Vantage Point' all take place 23 minutes before the assassination attempt on the president.

- W is the 23rd letter of the alphabet. Look at your keyboard. What numbers are directly above W?

CHAPTER NINE

THE 11:11 PHENOMENON

In this book so far we have covered the numbers one to nine. After nine comes ten, which is the first compound number. One and zero equals one. That brings us back to the number 1 and this symbolises that we are caught in a loop. It is the loop of birth and rebirth. But there's a way out of the loop, out of the cycle of birth and rebirth, and that is the number 11:11. Instead of the number ten bringing us back to the number one, we can choose to walk through the door of the 11:11. 11:11 is the number that embodies all numbers and is the key that opens the door to cosmic consciousness.

Put '11 11 phenomenon' into google and you'll get about 33 million pages to choose from. It's massive. All over the world people are noticing that the number 11:11 keeps appearing to them in their everyday life and they're all asking the same question; Why? What does it mean? Does it have a meaning or is it just coincidence?

As recently as ten years ago, hardly anybody had heard about the 11:11 phenomenon. Now there's an explosion of interest as it is touching the lives of more and more people. It's growing by the day, in a similar way that the appearance and knowledge of crop circles has grown over the years. In the 1980s I regularly saw crop circles in England but they were never reported in the press. Now crop circles are generally accepted as meaningful and authentic messages of consciousness. Interestingly, the 11:11 has appeared in some of the more recent crop circles.

Of all the numbers that could appear in your life, 11:11 is the most important.

11:11 represents a wake-up call. It's a pre-encoded trigger

within your cellular system telling you that it's time to become conscious of your true nature. Our brains are very large but we only use a small percentage of what we have. It's like having a computer with 5000MB but you only use 10GB. What a waste! When the 11:11 appears to you, you need to seize the opportunity that is being presented to you. 11:11 is all about transforming your consciousness. Are you ready for it? Are you ready to rock your world and discover the truth about your so called reality? Are you willing to let go of your selfish wants, needs and desires? Something new is trying to manifest in your life. You can choose whether to ignore it or embrace it.

Of course there are those who argue that it's only because 11:11 is a noticeable number that it is seen and that maybe a random number such as 378 is appearing just as frequently but we don't notice it. Try putting '378' phenomenon' into google and you won't find anything. Even using other repeated digits such as the '777 phenomenon' or the '33 33 phenomenon' also brings up nothing. Those phenomena don't exist. The two main number mysteries in the world at this present time are the 11:11 phenomenon and the 23 enigma.

Those who deny the existence of the 11:11 are those who are not yet at the receiving end of this number. When the 11:11 phenomenon hits you, you will then have no doubt that 11:11 has significance and is not just coincidental.

'As within, so without.' The 11:11 appearing in front of your eyes is an outer sign of an inner change within your DNA as you move into a higher frequency of consciousness. It indicates that your DNA is being transformed in preparation for the new consciousness that is manifesting on earth. This change will happen to more and more people as we fully enter the Age of Aquarius.

It is becoming a recognised fact that 11:11 appears in your life during a time of accelerated spiritual progress. However, I believe it is more than that. I think 11:11 can be used as a sign to direct you towards your unique spiritual path.

When you see the 11:11, you are being given an opportunity to merge with the One Consciousness. To do that, you have to give up your ego. That's the price of the ticket that you must pay to pass through the door. It sounds like a relatively easy thing to do, but it's not. At least I have not found it that easy! It depends on how powerful a grip your ego holds. The 11:11 sign is saying 'go for it'. It's rather like a finger pointing the direction in which you need to go in order to fulfil your mission on earth. You are being asked to bypass the judgements, analysis and thoughts of the lower mind. The 11:11 also asks you to put aside the wants, needs and desires of the ego. However, it is not asking you to bypass the intuition. Even if there are many 11:11 signs around a particular situation, if it doesn't *feel* right to me, then I won't act on it.

Following the 11:11 can require you to take huge leaps of faith. Let me give you an example.

I was looking for a property to use as a yoga centre. I found an old convent in Spain. I didn't like it. It was ancient, creepy and way beyond my budget. But the estate agent emailed me at 11:11, the church bells rang at 11:11 just as I was reading about the convent and the price was 111,100 euros. So I bought it. (*You can read the incredible story of my personal 11:11 wake-up call in my book The 11:11 Code.*)

To follow the 11:11 as a sign, as a way of leaving behind the wants, needs and desires of the ego requires courageous acts such as this. The mind needs to be kept out of the decision making. If I had allowed my mind to become involved in the decision to purchase this convent, I would never have bought it. It was ruined, having been uninhabited for more than 50 years and I could not afford the renovations. It simply didn't make sense, but then acts and decisions based on the 11:11 rarely do.

11 11 is a binary number. The binary system of numbers is expressed as a combination of 1's and 0's. We normally use the decimal system which is based on 10 numbers, 0 to 9. To convert

a decimal number to binary, the following chart can be used:

256	128	64	32	16	8	4	2	1
				1	0	0	0	1
				1	0	1	1	1
	1	1	0	0	0	0	0	1

Examples;
17 as binary is 10001 (16+1)
23 as binary is 10111 (16+4+2+1)
193 as binary is 11000001 (128+64+1)

You will recognise that the numbers on the top line are associated with computers. That is because computers operate with the binary system. It follows that a Divine intelligence could run on the same system.

A computer doesn't have an ego like most people have egos so on the whole they're pretty obedient to the programmer! When we put a programme into it a computer it normally does what we ask of it.

If we get our ego out of the way then the 11:11 code can work through us and guide us and we will be responding to God. God will be the programmer. I call it God but we could call it the One Consciousness or Universal Intelligence. When the programming is complete we will become Love in action.

All computers work on the same binary code system. We don't have French ones that work on one system or Australian ones that work on a different one. We are one Humanity, whatever our nationality, religion or sex. We all carry the same code. We have lost our connection to Divine Love but 1 by 1 we are re-connecting to our divinity. (And 1 and 1 are the first two numbers of the Fibonacci series of numbers......)

Another peculiarity of the number 11:11 is that it remains the same whichever way you look at it. You can turn it upside down, back to front, backwards or mirror image. It always looks the same. It is a number of perfect balance.

Then there is the indisputable fact that in many countries the only time the population pauses as one consciousness is on Armistice Day/Veterans day. Regardless of religion, sex, age or ethnic origin they pause at the 11th hour of the 11th day of the 11th month. This does not happen at Christmas, Eid, Easter, Divali or on other religious days, does it?

One day I am sure that all of Humanity will be familiar with 11:11 as a language of consciousness that links us together as One.

Questions and Answers

I look at the clock and notice that it says 11:11. Why does this happen so often? What makes me look at the clock at that very minute?

I do not believe this is by chance. Or coincidence. I believe that 11:11 is a spiritual code and when it starts appearing in your everyday life, it's your Higher Self telling you that it's time to wake up. It's great that you are noticing the 11:11 because now you can start working with it.

How can I work with it?

Whenever you notice the 11:11, be very aware of what you are doing in that moment. Or what you are thinking about. If you see the 11:11, pause, become aware of your surroundings and observe with clarity what is happening in that moment. Become 100% aware. Make a note of who you see, who texts you, who phones you, who calls at your door, or who you are with when you happen to see the 11:11 sign.

Some people have a difficult time linked to the 11:11 sign. Is it an evil number?

No it's not. The 11:11 will do what is necessary to rouse you from your current level of consciousness and being woken up isn't always a comfortable experience. The more you resist 'going with the flow' of 11:11, the more uncomfortable it will be.

I was born on 11/11. What does that mean?

Being born on 11th November at this particular time in the history of the earth suggests very strongly that at a soul level you want to become spiritually aware.

I have heard 11:11 is linked to 2012. Is it?

Add up the date of the winter solstice in 2012: 21.12.2012. It adds up to 11.

The solstice is the day the sun moves into Capricorn. On the 21.12.2012 that happens at exactly 11:11am Greenwich Mean Time.

I read that 11:11 has to do with portals opening. I don't understand what that means. Can you explain?

I didn't understand that either. I was experiencing all these 11:11s and friends were telling me to 'step through the portal'. How do you step through a portal? Where was this portal? I couldn't see a portal. That was far too obscure for me to understand! Now I understand what they meant by that. The 11:11 is opening a doorway within your consciousness. You 'step through it' by consciously agreeing that you are ready to leave selfishness behind. You agree to step up to your role on the planet, whatever that may entail.

That said, 11:11 is happening on a cosmic scale as well as in a personal way for Earth is, like us, a living being.

What is an 'elevener'?

An elevener is somebody who pauses for one minute at 11:11 each day and imagines a peaceful world. They realise that thoughts create reality and the more of us who contribute to that particular thought form, the greater the power of that thought.

CHAPTER TEN

THE LAW OF FIVE

5 is the number of both change and manifestation. We can use its power within the magic square to create change in our lives. To manifest, we use the law of 5. How? By creating a life list. On this list you write the 5 most pressing goals in your own life. Imagine you only had a year or two to live. What would you put on this list?

EXAMPLE

Visit my elderly auntie in Spain.
Learn to surf.
Climb Snowdonia.
Finish building the conservatory.
Resolve the conflict with my brother by apologising to him.

Once you have achieved something on your list, it is replaced with another goal. **There must always be exactly 5 things on the list.**

After a year the list might be:

Finish building the conservatory.
Spend a month surfing.
Climb Snowdonia.
Find some voluntary work.
Learn to sail.

You might change your mind about climbing Snowdonia. That's okay. Just cross it off and replace it with something else. You might learn to sail before you finish building the conservatory. That's okay too because you can tackle your list in any order.

Using the life list will help to keep you focussed and directed in this life. Using the knowledge of your own personal numbers can help you to decide what you put on the list.

B O O K S

O is a symbol of the world, of oneness and unity. In different cultures it also means the "eye," symbolizing knowledge and insight. We aim to publish books that are accessible, constructive and that challenge accepted opinion, both that of academia and the "moral majority."

Our books are available in all good English language bookstores worldwide. If you don't see the book on the shelves ask the bookstore to order it for you, quoting the ISBN number and title. Alternatively you can order online (all major online retail sites carry our titles) or contact the distributor in the relevant country, listed on the copyright page.

See our website **www.o-books.net** for a full list of over 500 titles, growing by 100 a year.

And tune in to myspiritradio.com for our book review radio show, hosted by June-Elleni Laine, where you can listen to the authors discussing their books.

MySpiritRadio